CAFFEINE,

NICOTINE,

AND

ADRENALINE

(from Nomex to Scrubs)

T. BROWN

ISBN: 978-1-71664-749-9

Caffeine, Nicotine, and Adrenaline

This book is dedicated to the following special people:

Horace and (in loving memory of) Barbara Ashford, my parents. They always said I could accomplish anything I set my mind too.

Chris Weber, Chief of the Dam Volunteer Fire Department. He believed even a 'girl' could be a Crew Boss and Engine Boss. He taught me so many life lessons I will carry with me always.

Earlene Shaw, L.V.N., thank you for 'pushing' me to be the top of my class. And for assigning me to a night shift with outstanding co-workers.

This is one woman's journey from wildland firefighter to Certified Nurse Assistant, and the life lessons learned from both career choices. Learning to believe in yourself and have self-confidence, no matter where your journey leads, is important. And showing other women they too can achieve their dreams, is a great accomplishment.

It is not always easy working in a male dominated career, but it can be accomplished and always remember, respect is earned, not merely given freely. You will be picked on and teased _____ it is all in how you handle it. A little sarcasm and a sense of humor can go a long way.

It did not hurt that I could be myself from the time I was a child and was always encouraged to try new things. Even though I have always been my own worst critic, I also pushed myself to succeed at whatever I was attempting. I was always a tomboy when I was young and was my father's shadow. He taught me how to work on my car, to fish and hunt, work construction as well as creativity. Throughout my life I have always had more male friends than female, maybe it was because there is less drama that way (sorry ladies, but it is true).

I have worked with many awesome men as well as women, and I have learned many lessons from both. One of the main things to remember is to always be yourself. You can learn from others, but you do not have to 'copy' them. Although many of us wear different 'hats', do not pretend to be someone you are not.

{ One }

When my family and I moved to Rochelle, Texas (yes, it is on the map} little did I know I would join the Rochelle Volunteer Fire Department. Prior to this move I did not even know volunteer fire departments existed. For most of my life I had lived in large cities with full time, paid fire departments. But, in 1999, at the age of thirty-nine, that is what I found myself doing, becoming a member of the volunteer fire department.

When I first became a member of the department, it was pure old-school. The 'paging' system was a solid ring on our home phones, back when everyone still had a landline. The 9-1-1 dispatcher would receive the initial emergency call, then call our department number. One of three members would answer, sometimes all three. The next step was to report to the station, literally around the corner from our house, and activate the outdoor siren, which was also used to alert the community to a tornado warning. My role consisted of answering the phone calls, activating the siren, and manning the station. Once the responding units arrived on scene a size-up would be reported, and once received I would assess what type of rehab supplies would be needed. If it was determined to be a large incident, I would begin the task of contacting local stores and restaurants for donations. Cases of water, Gatorade, snacks and at times fifty to sixty meals for all the responding departments. I would have my personal vehicle loaded and deliver supplies to the staging area of the incident. Living ten miles from a small city made obtaining donations an easy job. The grocery store, restaurants, as well as Walmart were always ready to help.

Volunteer fire departments run on fund-raisers held each year. After I had been a member for about one year the department officers began looking into applying for available grants. The grant money received would be used to purchase new equipment, apparatus, and wildland personal protective gear. There are specific guidelines, as well as deadlines to meet in order to receive grant monies. Therefore, the department voted to send me to Austin, Texas to attend a two-day course on

NFIRS (National Fire Incident Reporting System), a computer reporting system. For submission of some grants, all incidents, no matter the size need to be documented and submitted through NFIRS. For each incident I gathered the statistics, from size (acres burned) to number of department personnel and apparatus that responded.

The second class I attended, as well as most of the active members (those consistently responding to fire and/or other emergency calls), was the NOAA Skywarn Weather Spotter class. After receiving certificates, when severe weather called for it, we were paged out. Responders would report to dispatch, as well as the Emergency Operations Coordinator (E.O.C.). Any severe weather occurring in our response area, including hail, straight line winds, and tornado activity was reported.

During an active Spring weather occurrence, we had five weather spotters in various locations in our response area. Myself and two junior members manned the station. Radio transmissions were constant throughout the county. Reports included hail damage, trees down, and a confirmed tornado, which was headed for the community of Rochelle. It was up to me to drive up the road to the school cafeteria where they were holding a sports banquet, and alert them to the imminent tornado moving towards the community. I interrupted to tell the teachers in charge that all in attendance needed to be moved to the old gym, which was basically built underground. I actually had a grown man walk outside, look straight up and tell me, "I don't see any tornadoes."! At least the teachers took my advice and started moving everyone across the parking lot to the old gym.

I got back to the station before the sky turned pea green, the roar of the 'train' could be heard, and the hail started hitting the metal roof of the station. The tornado passed over the station, touching down just across the street. As the lightning struck, a bolt passed under the overhead door, under the tender (water tank truck) and back out. Although it occurred in a matter of seconds, watching it occur from across the station, it seemed to be in slow motion.

A call came across the radio, E.O.C. for Rochelle Station. A request was being made for a weather update from our response area. I responded, "Heavy rain, quarter size hail, small, brief tornado, and snow.". There was a brief silence on the radio, and I was asked to repeat my transmission, which I did, word for word. Once again, the radio went silent and the phone rang almost immediately. I answered and heard a man's voice on the other end, "Snow?!". I proceeded to explain to the E.O.C. that when the hail hit the roof of the station the blown-on insulation was knocked loose. It had 'snowed', covering everything in the station. I began laughing, and _____ he hung up on me! No matter what the situation, it is always good to find the humor in it.

The sky cleared and the weather spotters transitioned from spotting weather conditions to assessing the damage. The reports came in, downed trees and limbs, damage to roofs, and broken windows from the hail. Thankfully there were no injuries reported.

{ TWO }

New Year's Eve 2000, Y2K! The night all hell was supposed to break loose across the country. Computers of major companies, banks, and utilities were forecasted to shut down. Fire departments, law enforcement, and first responders were put on high alert. All fire departments were to be manned and ready to respond.

Taking shifts, the Rochelle Fire Department members manned the station throughout the night. Midnight _____ came and went. Members continued to man the station, playing cards, dominoes and waiting. The beginning of the New Year dawned without a single incident. So much for the predictions and hype!

****

When you live in a small, rural community most of your neighbors and fellow firefighters attend the same small church. On Easter Sunday we were all in attendance, pagers set to vibrate. Halfway through the service, pagers started going off! Apologizing as we got up to leave, the pastor simply said, "When duty calls, you must go. Stay safe.". Fires do not wait for you to be free to respond.

{ THREE }

As I became more involved with the department, Chief suggested that I attend the wildland fire academy. In February 2001, I found myself at the Central Texas Wildland Fire Academy, registered for Basic Wildland Firefighter. It lasted one very long week, and I was the only female in my class.

The first two days were spent in the classroom with the remaining three days outside for hands-on training. The first day outdoors we were instructed on the proper use and care of hand-tools, as well as the proper way to carry the tool while moving to the fire line. These tools included shovels, Pulaski's, and fire rakes (not your garden variety). We were told to grab a hand-tool of our choice and we moved out to the field single file. We began digging a handline (fire break), approximately two foot-wide across the field, continuing up to the top of a berm (a raised barrier between the field and a densely wooded area).

When we completed the handline, the instructor had us gather at the base of the berm, and I was then sent hiking back up to the top. I did as instructed, and then he yelled up to me, "How does it look?". That was the moment I figured out being a female in the fire service would have its own challenges. I hiked back down, marched right up to him and stated, "Looks good, are we done now?". He just smiled and dismissed the class for lunch break. I walked away feeling accomplished and even more determined to earn my certification.

The next two days in the field proved that there is never a dull moment, at least not when I am present! The fourth day of class was spent learning about different tools used to start a back burn. This is achieved by starting a controlled fire on the flanks or ahead of an advancing fire. This technique is used to slow the progression and/or stop the wildfire.

We were taught the proper use of different fire-starting devices, including drip torches, fuzees (flares), flare guns and a zip torch, which is a hand-held (small) device that fires a shell like a rifle. It ignites upon hitting the ground. No big deal, hold in one hand, pull the trigger back with my thumb, and release. Easy Peasy. The instructor placed his hand under mine and 'set' the aim. I pulled back the trigger, released, and it caught on my leather glove _____ not firing! Now, with glove removed, thinking my aim was exactly as he had it, I fired. All I remember is the look on his face, while making downward motions with both hands. He was frantically repeating, "Down, Down, Down!". If my aim had been just a little higher, it would have cleared the berm, igniting the wooded area beyond and we then could have practiced suppression, it fell just short. At the end of class that day our instructor handed me the shell casing. As a souvenir? Or maybe as a reminder of a close call?

Our last day of class would begin that morning with a controlled burn. We lined up across the end of the field and prepared to light the drip torches, the area we were to burn would stop at the handline we had cleared the prior morning. The instructor decided I should stick with him for this training. I got the feeling maybe he was just a tad nervous about me putting fire on the ground. He and I were positioned near the base of the berm, and all precautions were in place. Another Texas Forest Service employee was stationed at the top of the berm as our lookout, also providing weather condition updates. Two Type 6 Engines (brush trucks) were on stand-by, just in case they were needed.

The drip torches were lit, and we started moving forward, putting fire on the ground. There were taller, blue stem grasses along the base of the berm, it ignited and was burning slowly, as planned. Who knew that in the tall grass, which was now burning, was a skunk! It proceeded to run up the berm, straight toward our lookout! Luckily, for both, the skunk turned before reaching the top and the human standing there. I am happy (and relieved) to report that no humans were sprayed during this training _____ just another case of a close call.

That afternoon would be our final test, deploying and securing a fire shelter. This is a timed test in which you are given twenty-five seconds in which to remove the shelter from its case, shake it open, step into the corners and hit the ground. Once on the ground it should cover your entire body, held securely in place by your outstretched hands and legs/feet (at each corner). After this is accomplished, in the allotted time, an instructor walks the perimeter, pulling on the edges, to check if any of the shelter comes loose. However, when it came to me, three grown men pulled, tugged, and shook my shelter. It seemed as though a hurricane had hit unexpectedly! Being 5'3" does have its advantages! I was able to wrap the shelter completely underneath me. It was not coming loose!

At the end of the five long days, I received my Basic Wildland Firefighter certification. One week after returning home I was on my first fire incident, a 250-acre grass fire. Assigned to the back of a Type 6 Engine, nozzle in hand, and wildland firefighting in my blood.

{ FOUR }

September 11, 2001. A day all Americans will remember. We remember where we were, what we were doing, and who we were with on that tragic morning. The United States had been attacked by terrorists. When I heard the first report on the local radio station, I initially thought some 'idiot' had flown a small, personal jet into the tower. Seconds later my Dad called and told me to turn on my television. I turned it on just as the second plane hit the towers, I just sat down on my coffee table, in disbelief.

In the days that followed neighbors helped neighbors, strangers prayed together, and sent donations. Anyone who had one, or could obtain one, flew the American flag with a renewed pride of Country. The President called for all flags to be flown at half-staff to honor all of those who perished that day. In those days and weeks following September 11, it became almost impossible to purchase an American flag. Stores completely sold out, supply could not keep up with demand.

Two days after September 11, it occurred to me the Rochelle Fire Department did not have a flagpole. I started making phone calls and within the week I had a metal pipe donated and delivered. My Dad primed and painted it, and he and department members got it into place and erected. Through countless phone calls my Mom was able to locate and have an American flag delivered to the station.

On September 17, 2001 the Rochelle Fire Department members gathered at the newly installed flagpole. Chief Tom Bourbon raised the flag for the first time, and in honor of those lives lost, solemnly lowered it to half-staff

Never Forget!

{ FIVE }

Over the next three years I continued my firefighter training, attending two wildland fire academies a year. The Central Texas Wildland Academy, held for one week in February at Camp Bowie, Brownwood, Texas. The other, Capitol Area Interagency Wildfire Academy, held for two weeks in October at Camp Swift in McDade, Texas.

I completed Wildland Firefighter II, Fire Origin and Cause, Wildland Fire Investigation, as well as other certifications. The training took place in the classroom as well as hands-on in the field. However, there were plenty of lessons learned from the gatherings after classes. They came from the shared stories and experiences of the seasoned firefighters. All you had to do was listen and learn.

If you ever think you know everything about wildland firefighting _____ then maybe it is time to quit. Wildland fires are a constantly changing environment, including 'making' its own weather within the fire. Firefighting techniques and tools are also constantly changing and improving, therefore ongoing training is very important.

As with any camp or academy attended with friends (and firefighters) there was always jokes and pranks being played. Although I registered for the academies through my home department, I bunked with the members of the Dam Fire Department. Their department was provided a separate building since they assisted with the academy. All other attendees (except for the staff) stayed in General Population, in military style barracks.

Of course, with the name 'Dam' fire department there was always plenty of opportunities for a play on words. This included the department shirts, with the motto, "Best Fire Department by a Dam Site". Then there was the First Annual Dam 'Pool' Party. Okay, it was not an actual swimming pool, but a drop tank filled with water from the five-hundred-gallon tank on the Engine. Being late October, it was not warm water! Leave it up to the Academy Safety Officer to be the only one brave (or crazy) enough to go for a late evening swim. He did have on his red plastic, junior firefighter (children's) chief's helmet. Safety first!

As with most pranks, to be successfully pulled off you must be creative. My roommate and fellow firefighter, Ms. Mona, did just that. Everyone likes receiving potted plants and/or flowers. Therefore, it was decided that the Academy Medical Officer needed a little something for his Army green, drab desk. Rubber plants are always nice. So, after classes that day, off we went to the super center to purchase supplies. Once back at camp we sat for hours, stems, leaves, floral tape, and _____and created a 'rubber' plant (yes, that is what the 'flowers', in varying colors, was made from).

The next morning, we delivered it, in a real nice gift bag complete with tissue paper. Anonymously, or so we thought! We left the 'gift' on his desk after seeing him head for the Mess Hall for breakfast. We calmly walked into the Mess Hall and joined our crew for coffee. Needless to say, we hurried to class when we heard our names being called down classroom row! So much for being anonymous!

Being late October and knowing your roommate is terribly afraid of spiders _____ the temptation can just be too great. All of the stores had Halloween decorations on display, so it was not difficult finding a large rubber tarantula! That night while she was in the bathroom getting ready for bed, the spider was strategically placed. Tucked in underneath her cozy blankets, in just the right spot at the foot of her bed. I climbed into my bunk, pulled up the covers, turned to face the wall and waited. She came into our room, sat down on the edge of her bunk, kicked off her shoes and climbed into bed. Pulling up her covers, she stretched her right leg out (like I was betting she would) and her foot touched the large spider. She proceeded to come unglued! The guys, awakened by her screams, came rushing into our room. Not knowing what to expect, they all had a good laugh after the 'intruder' was found. For some reason, maybe because I could not stop laughing, she immediately blamed me!

******

Among inside jokes shared were the restaurant closings. These occurred in the nearest town to the academy. Was it only a coincidence that they closed after an academy had been held? Could it have been a table shared by six plus firefighters, enjoying drinks and dinner, maybe having a little too much fun. Those that were present in the vehicle (on the way to dinner) know of the encounter with 'Trigger', and the laughter that ensued! The restaurant closed shortly after the academy.

It was probably a shear fluke that an Asian restaurant closed after academy attendees had dinner there (not the same year as the above). I believe it was just happenstance, closing after academies. At least that is my story and I am sticking to it!

******

As 2003 came to an end there was no doubt that firefighting was in my blood. I now had an extended family. It was also evident that some major life changes were coming in 2004. Due to a separation and impending divorce I resigned from the Rochelle Fire Department in March 2004. The next month I moved to Austin, Texas. I did continue my fire training, attending the academy later that year in October.

{ SIX }

In the Spring of 2005, I took a giant leap and moved North of the Mason-Dixon line, to Pennsylvania. The first year I was there I worked as a security guard. Then I got the phone call, an interview was set up with the Pennsylvania Department of Conservation and Natural Resources (DCNR). I had scored a ninety-eight percent on the wildland firefighter exam, taken at the time I submitted my application.

The interview was conducted by three employees, including the District Chief. After an hour of interview questions, I was asked if I had anything I wanted to ask them. I stated that I thought everything had been covered. Just when I thought it was concluded, one gentleman said he had one more question. It was regarding one of my references I had listed, a Texas Forest Service employee. I was trying to figure out where this was leading, but I confirmed to him, that yes, he was a burn specialist with the Texas Forest Service. There was a moment of silence as he flipped through my application again. He looked up at me and stated, "I thought so!". He proceeded to tell me that he once had to take over teaching a class at Emmitsburg, Maryland. The Texas Forest Service had called him back to Texas for a fire assignment.

The interview was over, and I was dismissed. We shook hands and I left, wondering if I would even hear from them. Early the next morning I received a phone call, the voice on the other end asking, "Do you want to work for DCNR?". Well _____ Yes! I was being given the opportunity to work my dream job! The next morning, I reported to my assigned station, I was now a seasonal wildland firefighter for the State of Pennsylvania.

I arrived the first day to an empty station, No crew, No engines, completely alone. Within a few minutes the District Chief arrived and informed me, "We are going to break you in right, we have a fire.". He then turned, without another word and walked into the station. I just shrugged my shoulders and returned to my car to grab my gear bag and helmet. We met back at his truck, he was holding a pair of leather gloves and a helmet.

With a surprised look on his face, he realized I had my own gear. We loaded up and headed to the fire incident.

Upon arriving on scene a few quick introductions were made with my crew, I grabbed a hand-tool and went to work. I also located the cause and point of origin, not bad for the first day on the job.

By the time the fire was contained and was into the mop-up stage it was midafternoon. It was time for a break, we gathered around the engines and grabbed a bottle of water. Paying more attention to the job at hand up to this point in time, I now realized I was the only female on my crew. Even though I had worked side by side with these men for most of the day it was now time to 'prove' myself, as the following conversation took place.

Firefighter 1: "So, you are from Texas?".

I told him, "Yep, I am".

Firefighter 2: "So where did you get your training?".

I simply told him, "From the best, the Texas Forest Service.".

Firefighter 1: "What was the biggest fire you were on?".

I asked him to clarify, "Do you mean the last or the largest?".

He then asked, "What is the difference?".

I proceeded to tell him, "About 12,000 acres"!

Check _____ Mate! I had proven myself as a wildland firefighter with just one conversation. The next morning, I was assigned my Type 6 Engine!

Another optional part of our job was attending special events, as Smokey Bear. I did this on two occasions, the second being an outdoor car show, in the middle of Summer, and the hottest day of the year in Pennsylvania. I also came to realize the Smokey Bear costume was not exactly made for a short person. At least there was a small event center on site with a walk-in freezer! I was making good use of it about every thirty to forty-five minutes. All the children's smiles and hugs made it all worthwhile.

{ SEVEN }

There were many lessons learned throughout the three seasons (mid-March through mid-November) I worked in Pennsylvania. The first, there is no flat land up there. We pulled one-inch hose for suppression and put hand-tools to use. There was no firefighting from a rolling brush truck. I was also introduced to using an Indian tank. A five-gallon (approximately forty pounds) water tank with an attached low-pressure hand-held nozzle. It is carried on your back, like a backpack, and is primarily used for mop-up. I had to ask twice, to make sure I had heard correctly, the first time I was told to go get the leaf blower from the engine! Not a tool you would use in Texas, unless of course you wanted the outcome to be a larger incident! It proved to be a great tool for clearing a line and containing a fire in the mountains of Pennsylvania, where the terrain is covered with three to six inches of duff (decomposed leaves, plants, and pine needles.

I also continued with my training in Pennsylvania, where I registered for a Chainsaw course. After learning care and maintenance of chainsaws, it was time for some hands-on training in the field. We were assigned a tree to be cut down, then we had to tell the instructor where we would make our cuts on the tree and where it would fall. He marked the spot we indicated with a stake, and we felled our tree. I was very surprised and felt accomplished when my tree fell within five inches of the stake! Again, I was the only female in class, nothing new there, but I placed in the top three of the class.

I learned what it was like to watch for smoke and/or fires from a Fire Tower, we each rotated through a schedule of spending a day on duty in the Fire Tower. Although I did not have any sightings to report, the view from that height was spectacular.

The harshest lesson I learned was discovering that hornets built their nests just under the topsoil. Who knew?! I found out the hard way, when I stepped on top of one. We were pulling cut tree limbs off a dirt road in a State Park. As I stepped back onto the road, I felt the first sting. When I looked down, my pants legs were covered in small hornets, as well as my arms, chest, and back. My immediate reaction was to brush them off and get away from the area. Luckily, I had a t-shirt on, so I proceeded to quickly get my long-sleeved work shirt off. After arriving home, I lost count at one hundred stings as I applied Benadryl. Only my face, hands, and feet had escaped being stung. Luckily, I had no serious side effects from the incident other than the major pain in my arms and some swelling. But I am now highly allergic to any type of bee, wasp, or hornet sting.

It was in the middle of my third season I sustained a serious injury to my left wrist. I was using an Indian tank, working mop-up, when I lost my footing. Having the nozzle in my right hand I attempted to brace my fall with my left. What I could not see was the large rock covered in duff. I knew it was injured and needed to be stabilized, so I hiked back up to my engine. I proceeded to tape it (finding only a roll of electrical tap _____ improvise, adapt, and overcome), and I was getting my leather gloves back on when our (station) Chief approached me. I explained what had occurred and he asked if I needed to go have it checked. First, there were three or four engines parked behind mine, what was he going to do, move them? So, I replied, "Just help me get my Indian tank back on, there is work to finish, I will go get it checked when we clear the incident." That is when he discovered just what 'Texas Tough' meant!

I eventually made it to the emergency room (eight hours later) dirty, tired, and hungry. I was finally called back to an exam room, two hours after my arrival. X-rays taken, wrist stabilized in an air cast, pain killer injected, I was released.

Stopping only for a drive-thru hamburger, I arrived home at midnight. The next morning, I reported to my station, air cast and all. I was assigned to station duty, since you cannot very well fight fire one-handed. After one week (and a very clean station), the District Chief arrived at the station and told me, "We need to talk.". After beginning the conversation with 'I don't like this, and I know you are not going to either', I was told I was being placed on paid medical leave. I did not like it, but I understood why, and it was better than the first thought I had, 'he is going to fire me'!

After a month of physical therapy, with no improvement, I was referred to an Orthopedic Specialist. I spent the next month in a hard splint until an MRI could be scheduled. Due to the ligament and tendon damage shown on the MRI, my arm from palm to above the elbow was put in a traditional cast. The Doctor did not want any movement in my wrist area. I spent the next year in varying casts and braces, as the Doctor was hoping it would heal without surgery. By the end of that year, I had decided I had had enough of the Northeast, not to mention the snow! I began planning my move back to Texas.

In mid-February 2009 I left Pennsylvania headed for Virginia to spend time with my daughter. That May I made my final trip back to Pennsylvania, a doctor's appointment was my first stop. Even though it was still painful to use my hand, I convinced him it was better, and I got my medical release. I was instructed to begin physical therapy once I arrived back in Texas. I made one other stop, to turn in my resignation to DCNR. It had been a long, busy day, and was now raining. I made the decision to stop for the night at a hotel just North of the Mason-Dixon line. The next morning dawned with a clear blue sky and dry roads, I headed back to Virginia Beach, never looking back. I stayed with my daughter until July of that year.

The morning of July 7, with my Blazer loaded to the roof, me and my new pup, Maggie, headed for Texas. Two and a half days later I pulled into Rochelle. You can take the girl out of Texas, but you cannot take Texas out of the girl, I was home!

{ EIGHT }

Only my immediate family knew that I had moved back to Texas. Keeping that a secret for three months was not an easy task for me! But it was worth the surprise when I showed up unexpectedly at the academy that October. It was fantastic reuniting with fire family and friends, and they were even more surprised to learn I was not just visiting but had moved back permanently. I mentioned that my position in Pennsylvania would be held open for three years, but I also made it clear, I was not leaving Texas again.

When the fire academy rolled around the following February I was there. Although I did not take any classes I worked check-in as well as anywhere help was needed. The next week I was back on a Type 6 Engine with the Dam Crew. We assisted the Texas Forest Service on an Rx (prescribed) burn at Camp Bowie, just outside of Brownwood, Texas.

2010 proved to be a busy year for me. I found a house in Brownwood, and me and Maggie (my pup) moved in that March, and I became a full-time member with the Dam Volunteer Fire Department. When officer elections came up that Fall, I was nominated and elected Training Officer. I took care of registering members for the academy in October, including my youngest daughter, who had joined the department. She received her Basic Wildland Firefighter certification and I became a certified Crew Boss and Engine Boss.

As Training Officer, I was in charge of planning and holding a training session once a month at the station. Everything from 'essentials to carry in your gear bag' to SCBA (Self-contained Breathing Apparatus) was covered. When new members joined the department, we would hold a general training meeting, which included filling out paperwork, issuing gear, and covering department guidelines and protocols. At one such meeting (addressing protocols) I asked the new members if they were aware of 'sexual harassment in the workplace'. They all assured me they were with a nod of their heads. That is when I informed them (in a very serious manner) "Here at the Dam Fire Department, sexual harassment (pausing for effect) is expected and will be graded.". With shocked looks on their faces, they immediately looked from me to Chief. They were attempting to figure out if this was just a joke. Without missing a beat, he remarked, "She is the Training Officer, I would listen to her.". We could only hold our laughter in for so long seeing the puzzled looks on their faces. I finally set their minds at ease and told them, "Just kidding!".

I also took care of planning the staff dinner held during the academy in February. It was attended by the Dam Fire Department members and Texas Forest Service employees, co-sponsors of the academy. Along with dinner, a special presentation was given by a Texas Forest Service employee, two consecutive years. They included a well-prepared power point as well as visual aids. All in attendance received certificates of participation for 'Oreo 101' and 'The Life and Death of a Twinkie'. The visual aids did not last long as the attendees ate them! But I am sure they proudly framed and displayed their certificates. Okay, I am sure they filed them away _____somewhere.

{ NINE }

2011 was the year of Texas burning. It started one Saturday in April for our department. Chief was picking me up to go to a fundraiser for another volunteer department in our county. When he pulled into my driveway, I was ready, I grabbed my gear bag, tossed it into the back and climbed in the front seat. Glancing back at my bag, he commented, "You really think you need that?". I simply replied, "I would rather have it and not need it, than need it and not have it.". He trained me well, it proved to be a good decision. We were not even halfway to the fundraiser when the tones dropped. We headed for the station, never making it for a hamburger.

The fire had been ignited in heavy brush by tracer bullets being used by the Army National Guard during training. Including suppression, mop-up, and patrolling the perimeter for hot spots we were on the incident for nine days. We spent fourteen to sixteen hours a day on the scene.

Along with numerous responding departments, Texas Forest Service crews and bulldozers, we had assistance from two retardant drop planes and two helicopters with Bambi buckets dropping water. By the end of the incident I informed Chief I would not be going with him for a hamburger anytime soon!

This was the beginning of a very long, busy fire season. Not only for our department and departments across Texas, but the Texas Forest Service as well. In the few days between large fire incidents we were either being paged out to small fires or on standby at the station. Two of the smaller fires were ignited by welding on fences. The conditions were so dry that it did not take but a small spark to start a fire.

The next large incident occurring in our immediate response area was the Circle P Fire. It was started by a housekeeper using a leaf blower and dropping a lit cigarette in very dry conditions. The main concern was the homes in the area threatened by the growing fire. The wind shifted and the fire jumped the main (farm to market) road, burning toward the Baptist Encampment.

There were approximately three hundred adults and children attending the camp. An evacuation was ordered, and all the neighboring school districts sent school buses to assist. Everyone was safely evacuated, and the fire was stopped before reaching the encampment. Only one structure, a storage shed, was lost. It seemed we were responding to a fire call every other day that summer. We were also receiving Mutual-Aid calls to assist other departments in our county as well as being paged out to assist on fires in other counties.

September began with a phone call from Chief. I was instructed to pick a crew and be ready to deploy in less than twenty-four hours. He had received a request for our assistance, we were headed for the Bastrop Complex Fire, just outside of Bastrop, Texas. I notified the two additional members that would make up our crew, my youngest daughter and Ms. Mona. Calls were made to those members who would be manning the station and responding to any local incidents in our absence. It was time to pack, check our gear, line up someone to take care of pets, and calls to family. The next morning, we headed to

Bastrop. Chief and my daughter in the Type 6 Engine, myself and Ms. Mona in my RAV, with all our gear and bags.

In the end 38,000 acres had burned, approximately 1600 homes were lost. Including homes belonging to firefighters battling the wildfire. Amazingly for an incident of this magnitude only two lives were lost.

The second morning waiting outside of the Command Post for Chief to get our assignment, a gentleman approached us. Like so many, he and his family had been evacuated to a hotel and he was attempting to find out any information about his home and neighborhood. We informed him that we were not from the local area and had traveled from Brown County. As we stood there talking, he told us about his family, three children including a three-year-old, who was only concerned about his Thomas the Train. It was apparent as he spoke with us that he was very thankful they were all safe.

On the drive home we realized we had never learned his name, only that he was a coach at a Bastrop school. With certainty we did know one thing, there was a little boy who needed Thomas the Train. We were on a mission, and the first step was finding out the name of the coach and his family. Through countless phone calls and emails, Ms. Mona learned who he was as well as the ages of his children, two boys and a girl. Our mission went into full swing. We spread the word that we were wanting to help this family and the residents of Bastrop that had lost so much to the fire. The community stepped up and donations began coming into the department. Ms. Mona and I went in search of Thomas the Train, buying everything we could.

By early December we had put together large shopping bags, one for each family member, and one very special shopping bag for a three-year-old. We also had many donations and gift cards to take to Bastrop for the members of the community.

Next came the delivery, three personal SUV's loaded with donations and our support vehicle, just in case anything happened along the way. We met at seven a.m. on December 21, the Dam Elves Christmas run was on the road. Who better to help Santa deliver than _____ firefighters? The school counselor helped in getting 'our' family to the Heart of the Pines fire station, without divulging the real reason behind the meeting. As we introduced ourselves you could see in his face that he remembered talking with us during the incident. We gave them their shopping bags full of individualized gifts, and the look on their faces and tears of joy were priceless. We explained how the story he had shared with us, of his little boy and a concern for Thomas the Train, had tugged at our hearts. We knew we had to help Santa deliver.

It had been a long day on the road as well as the excitement of seeing one family's appreciation for what we had accomplished. The whole experience made it one of the best Christmas' for us all. It reminded us, giving is much more gratifying than receiving.

{ TEN }

I have been on fire calls in all types of terrain, from the mountains of Pennsylvania to the flat land of Texas. For the most part I was in the hill country of Central Texas. I have been in parts of rural areas I never thought I would see. There were more than a few times that someone said, "If you hear duelin' banjos, drive faster!". When you come across a section of wire fence strung between two trees with a cow bell on it, and no other fencing _____ you stop and wonder, "What the heck?". Or a house that looked more like a shanty, with surveillance cameras up on the corner! In the backwoods, in the middle of nowhere, I do not think they were there to capture pictures of the wildlife.

For the most part we were either driving across pastures and wooded areas or on a two-track (one-lane dirt road). There were times you hit the brakes and asked, "Where did the road go?!". When the two-track seemed to disappear because of a steep drop-off, down around a tree at the bottom and back up the other side.

There were times (especially at night) that a 'spotter' on foot was needed ahead of the engine. Sometimes that does not help. One night I had a spotter ahead to talk me through a dry creek bed with a pretty good drop off. He radioed back to me and asked if I was comfortable driving across the creek. I let him know, "Not really"! We switched places and he got the engine across the creek. I cannot say if it was at that point or some other that night, but the entire back bumper of the engine came up missing! Another department found it the next day and let Chief know it was at their station.

I know you have heard the expression, 'stuck between a rock and a hard place', well in one instance it was 'stuck between two small Mesquite trees'! My crew and I were driving the black areas of a fire, checking for hot spots. My daughter asked if she could drive the engine, I agreed to let her, after all what could happen? Somehow, she managed to get the engine stuck between two small trees. She wanted me to take over and get it unstuck. I shook my head and told her no, she got it there, she could get it out. The other firefighter on the engine got off, and with him on one side and me on the other, we folded in the side mirrors and pulled the trees back as far as we could, thankfully they were small, young trees. She was finally able to back it out and get it unstuck. I took over driving the engine from that point.

{ ELEVEN }

There are several sayings I learned while in the fire service that have stayed with me to this day, and always will. They come in handy in day to day living.

Improvise, adapt and overcome. Preplanning is great, but even when things have the best laid plans, it does not always work out accordingly. Learning to improvise and adapt to situation, as well as overcome the obstacles that may deter you helps to make life less stressful. When you apply these three things you can often accomplish what you thought you might not be able too. It became a natural daily process for me.

There are three things that keep many firefighters alert and going, caffeine, nicotine, and adrenaline (as the title says).

Caffeine, a.k.a. coffee, is a must. Of course, it is a daily necessity for me, no matter what I am doing. Fresh brewed, bottled, canned, or instant (last resort), as long as it is not decaf. Decaf is just a waste of water. Hot or cold, if it is strong, just not strong enough to melt Styrofoam cups and/or plastic spoons but does not resemble weak tea. I have even known some firefighters to eat instant coffee! Yuck! Something I just never could bring myself to do.

Nicotine saves lives, okay maybe not mine, but definitely others that are hard to deal with tactfully! While on the fire line I once had a young, rookie firefighter asks me, "Why do firefighters smoke?". I thought it was a joke until I saw the serious look on his face. So, I proceeded to explain, "Firefighters are not always on a fire incident, therefore, to keep up the level of smoke intake in their system they light up.". He thought about that for a minute, and in all seriousness replied, "That makes sense.". My daughter almost fell off the engine laughing at my explanation and his response! I would like to say he was smarter than that _____ but I cannot. I would like to say my sarcasm came from being around firefighters, but again _____ I cannot. I believe I was born with it!

Finally, adrenaline. It is a natural process for the levels to increase when you are faced with a very stressful and/or an emergency situation. The important thing to learn is how to keep it under control. Thus, avoiding the possibility of making the situation worse. I told new members, "It is better to get there in one piece, than not get there at all".

Volunteer firefighter are allowed to have lightbars on their personal vehicles. It does not exempt them from any driving laws, and it is a personal choice. I for one, never felt the need to have a lightbar on my SUV. For some, it really is not a good idea.

Responding to the station I witnessed one of our younger members blatantly ignore several traffic laws, exceeding posted speed limits and running a four-way stop sign. I was very upset with him! I was told that upon arriving at the station I made it from my vehicle to him in three steps! Hard to believe, I am only 5'3"! Knowing I was mad, he tried to step behind Chief, but was immediately told, "You pissed her off, you are on your own!". I proceeded to inform him in no uncertain terms that if I ever witnessed that kind of driving again, I would get my Pulaski and personally smash his lightbar to tiny bits! He tried to tell me he would call the police if I did, I told him, "Go right ahead, by the time they get here, that light bar will be on the ground in a million tiny pieces". End of discussion!

If drivers will not pull over and give the right of way to emergency vehicles with lights and siren blaring, they are not going to for a pickup truck with a lightbar. About ninety percent of our calls were for wildland fires, no structures threatened. We may save a squirrel's home, but that is not worth putting yourself and others in danger. Too many younger members must be taught how to control the adrenaline rush that occurs when the tones drop. The ones who have been on a department for a while, listen to the call, head for the station, and arrive safely.

One of my favorites sayings is 'Better to beg for forgiveness than ask for permission'. At times you have to step-up and make a split-second decision, knowing there is a possibility of it not being the right choice. Although I might have had to explain my actions, I can honestly say, I have never begged for forgiveness due to my decision.

There are times that not asking permission works to your benefit.

One example of this saying involved the Dam dog. When your department does not have the traditional Dalmatian, the Chief's Pitbull becomes the mascot. The Chief and I were at the station getting things prepared to attend the academy when the discussion occurred. It came to my mind that the Dam dog (Charlie) needed to go to the academy. Chief did not agree! We threw 'yes he does' and 'no he doesn't' back and forth for a good hour. Chief finally told me that if I got permission than Charlie could go. Then I gave my final argument, I stated, "I was taught to beg for forgiveness, don't ask for permission.". Charlie went to the academy! Not only did he go, he was invited to attend the afternoon Staff meeting!

******

At times, with any human interaction miscommunications can occur, which is why repeating a received radio transmission is a good practice. By doing this it is confirmed that it is correct and understood (clearly) by those involved.

There was a miscommunication that occurred while my engine was in staging. My hand-held radio was in the engine and me and my crew were all outside of it getting drinks and food. A firefighter from another department approached me and told me that my Chief was attempting to contact me. He then proceeded to give me the message, "He wants you to sling _____ leather?". Sling leather?! "I think you mean sling Weather.". Slinging weather means to get and report the latest weather conditions, temperature, relative humidity, and wind speed and direction. He said, "I was not going to question it, I am just relaying the message.". As he walked away, I had to control my laughter before I could report the weather over the radio!

Another lesson you learn is to never say the "Q" word. As in 'it sure has been 'quiet' around here'. The minute that word is uttered, all hell is going to break loose. It never fails!

******

While on the fire line it is very important to stay hydrated. Not only do you have the heat from the fire itself but in Texas it can very well be 100 degrees or higher in the summer. It is also important to eat and keep your body fueled. We all carried non-perishables in our packs, small can fruit, granola bars, among other high protein items. We included plasticware, wet wipes and any personal items we might need. I also had one rule on my engine, for every Gatorade consumed, two bottles of water were to follow. Consuming only a thirst quencher type fluid can mess up a person's electrolytes.

One lesson you learn is that when sack lunches (with a sandwich included) were provided, let's just say _____ I sure hope you like mustard! You do not want mayonnaise; it will spoil in the heat. So, it is either mustard or dry. If it came down to it, we had MRE's (meals ready to eat) on every engine. By the end of a long incident most of those were missing the instant coffee and sugar packets. I always kept a supply of Vienna sausages and/or snack crackers in my pack. I just could not eat a cold MRE!

{ TWELVE }

Most everyone on the department had a nickname. It was not just assigned but was 'earned' at some point in time. 'Iceman' suffice it to say had nothing to do with Top Gun! And then there was 'My Little Pony', which was earned from a remark he made on a fire incident. When we pulled the engine into staging there was a Shetland pony tied to the side mirror of the department Suburban, our rehab vehicle. The remark was made, and the nickname stuck.

As for me, I had two, 'Rooski', not even real sure where it came from, and the Dam Bytch! I do know that one came from our Chief during an academy. I was working check-in and had a very impatient attendee wanting to cut in line, when I explained he would have to get in the line and check-in like everyone else, he went and asked Chief, "Who do I talk to about checking in?". Chief pointed my way and informed him, "The Redhead". The guy told him I was 'rude', and well, my nickname was earned! It could have also been because I once told a young member of the department that was assigned to my engine, "If you do not pay attention and you screw up, I will personally pull you off the fire line and drive you to the gate, drop you off and you can walk home.". It is too dangerous to not pay attention and do as assigned. He complained to Chief and was told, "She can, and she will.".

Sometimes nicknames were from an incident, sometimes from something said or done by that person. But it was always in good fun.

{ THIRTEEN }

There is some down time in the fire service, and much of ours was spent with the crew at Chief's home. Burgers on the grill, cold drinks, homemade ice cream churning, and stories shared around the fire pit, lasting late into the night.

Stories that were shared of experiences on and off the fire line. Like the first time chief told me to grab a drip torch and go start a back burn to contain a fire. "By myself?!". Hearing the stress in my voice, he encouraged me, telling me I knew what to do and I would be fine. Drip torch in hand I headed for the engine that would take me to the area to start the backburn. As I headed to the engine, I was going over in my mind what I needed to do to accomplish the task at hand. I heard Chief coming up behind me and when I turned around, there he was, drip torch in hand! He was not joining me out of concern, he just liked laying fire on the ground too much to miss the chance. There is a little pyromaniac in all of us (firefighters).

Or the first academy my daughter attended, convincing her there would be a 'major' test at the end of her Basic Wildland Firefighter class. She participated in class, took notes, and studied. On the final afternoon of class, when the instructor passed out papers, she asked if it was the test. Her being told it was just a survey about the academy, there was no test _____ Priceless! Not so much the look on her face when she located me, but it was still funny.

Chief shared stories of fire incidents that occurred before most of us were with the department. The fire that occurred on an island located on Lake Brownwood. Lake patrol ferried them and their gear over to the island. It was not inhabited, so basically it was a 'let it burn' type of incident. After all it was surrounded by water and would burn itself out. During the incident a boat pulled up near the island. A woman onboard was yelling and complaining, "Why aren't you getting a bulldozer out here and putting out the fire?". What part of 'it is an island' did she not get?!

Or telling of the call that was not broadcast over the radio. Dispatch paged our department making a request for Chief to call on the phone. While my daughter and I waited at home to hear what was going on, my phone rang. Chief informed me that we had a call, just around the corner from the station, children locked in a bedroom. My daughter and I took the call and headed to the residence. Upon arriving, sure enough there were two small children locked in a bedroom. However, the lock was on the hallway side of the door! No, this was not a prank or a joke. You cannot make this kind of stuff up! We unlocked the door, the children were fine.

Anyone in the fire service can attest to the fact that your crew becomes your second family. More than once birthdays were celebrated at Chief's house, burgers, cake and homemade ice cream. Of course, Charlie (the Dam dog) was always present. And when someone got side-tracked while serving ice cream, and left it unattended, Charlie helped himself!

{ FOURTEEN }

Once firefighting gets in your blood, it stays with you for life. Anytime there is a smoke column off in the distance you will go into firefighter 'mode'. You are going to watch it and try to size it up. You will listen to the scanner. Is 'your' department being paged? You will wait and listen for the initial size-up and who is responding.

But, then reality hits, you are not as young as you used to be *coughing* hard to admit sometimes. You have sustained injuries over the past fourteen years, any new injuries will not heal quite as quickly. You realize it has come time to hang up your helmet and move on, while you are still (for the most part) able to move. It has come time for the younger members to take the lead.

I still miss the comradery with fellow firefighters, and the sound of the pager going off at all times of the day and night. Okay, the pager, maybe not so much.

{ FIFTEEN }

The beginning of my next life adventure came about in January 2016. My 56th birthday present to myself _____ registering for a Certified Nurse Assistant course. It was being offered at a local nursing home, at no expense to the student.

Me! The one who always said, "I could never, ever work in a nursing home.". But here I was, taking my seat at the front of the classroom, and clearly the oldest student. Sitting right in front of the instructor proved to be entertaining at times. I was only a few years younger than she was, which meant I understood the 'looks' on her face at the questions and comments made by some of the younger students. By the end of the first week four students had quit the class. It clearly is not for everyone.

The second day of class began at six a.m. As I was heading to the classroom, I had just passed a resident when I heard, "Hey", I stepped back beside him and asked what he needed. Sitting in his Gerry Walker, he looked up at me with a very mischievous grin and _____ patted his lap! I simply told him, "Not today, I have to go to class.". Second day of class and I get 'hit' on by a ninety-year-old man!

Not only were the class expenses covered, we would be working for the nursing home. By the end of the first week we were assigned to our rotations. Most of the girls were requesting day shift, for one reason or another. So, when the instructor looked at me, I replied, "Day or night shift, I am single and as long as my dogs are fed, they do not care.". I was assigned to the night shift, 6 p.m. to 6 a.m. We would be working as 'Student' C.N.A.'s until we completed the course and passed the State Exam. This meant we would be assigned to a hall and work with a licensed C.N.A.

Night shift _____ if you think they all just sleep at night _____ Think again! The caffeine intake was about to increase. Mine, not theirs!

SIXTEEN

As class progressed, we practiced hands-on skills, taking vitals, lift assists, putting ted (compression) hose on, and repositioning a resident while they were in bed. We practiced on each other or the resident mannequin. I will be the first to admit, putting ted hose on a mannequin with a 'floppy' ankle joint is not easily accomplished, but I did finally succeed.

We also began learning lift assists using gate belts, stand and twist, and mechanical Hoyer lifts. With the Hoyer lift, we each took a turn at being lifted off the bed and back down. When it came to my turn to be the 'patient', they positioned the sling underneath me, attached it to the lift and I crossed my arms over my chest (the way a resident would be asked to do). When they started the lift, I flung my arm out to the side. They stopped the lift and told me to 'quit it'. I placed my arm back on my chest and once again they started the lift. Again, I flung my arm out to the side. Again, they stopped the lift, however it was our instructor (attempting not to laugh) who told me to stop. When they completed the lift, the girls asked me why I kept doing that. I simply pointed down the hall and said, "In a perfect world ......". Not all residents are going to calmly cross their arms and remain still.

I really believe my age and life experiences were beneficial to becoming a C.N.A. We had a resident paralyzed from the neck down, and he rarely had visitors. His call light (activated by blowing into a tube) was constantly being turned on. One morning in class one of the girls was complaining about how often she had to answer his call light the previous night. Before our instructor could say anything, I spoke up. I asked that student to sit on her hands. No matter what I said next, do not move her hands. I proceeded to tell her, "Oh my gosh, your nose is itching really bad." Reminding her to continue to sit on her hands. "Your nose is itching so much.". The power of persuasion can be very convincing, she tried to wiggle her nose. I told her and the others, "Now you have had a very small taste of his daily life! Not being able to do simple things that we all take for granted.". Their perspective was changed after they were made to think about it. Our instructor just smiled and nodded her head at me.

One hour of our daily class time was spent on the floor shadowing a (licensed) C.N.A. I will never forget the first call light I answered on my own, the C.N.A. was busy helping another resident. Knowing I could not assist the resident without a C.N.A. present, I could at least find out what they needed and report it back to her.

I entered the room, which was occupied by two women, both in their late eighties. They had been best friends since they were young children, and now were roommates at the nursing home. Emily, who was a total assist (Hoyer lift) and suffered from dementia had pushed the call button. She proceeded to tell me, "You girls are going to make me late!". I calmly told her we would be in to get her dressed and up in just a few minutes. Again, she complained that she was going to be late (for work, she had been a school bus driver). Before I could reply, her roommate, Hazel, spoke up, "You haven't worked in forty years!" Emily responded to her, "You don't know what you are talking about.". Hazel, shaking her head, "And just how are you going to get there?". Emily informed her, "My car is right outside, if I hadn't taken a wrong turn I wouldn't be here now!". The lead C.N.A. found me in the hall just outside their room, trying to contain my laughter. But when I told her about their conversation, we both started laughing. We all need a best friend, if for no other reason than to be roommates in a nursing home. At least one could 'keep it real'!

Four months after beginning the class I was headed to Waco, Texas to take my state exam. The first half of the test was one hundred multiple choice questions. In order to take the clinical (hands-on) portion of the exam you had to pass the written part. Myself and two of my classmates passed the written section, and we were called back that afternoon for the clinicals. I was paired with one of my classmates, we would take turns being the 'patient' and the other being the C.N.A. and then switch places. You must complete four out of five tasks assigned by the tester, and as the 'patient' you cannot say anything to correct or help the 'C.N.A.', I was proud of myself when I was informed I had successfully completed the assigned tasks. I was now a licensed C.N.A. in the State of Texas.

It turned out that being the 'patient' proved to be 'painful'. My classmate/ partner correctly washed her hands, one out of five tasks accomplished! And suffice it to say, you really should not attempt to correct the tester.

Before beginning the two-hour drive home, I texted my instructor and let her know I had passed. I was scheduled to work the next night, and so began three nights of orientation, working on a hall with another C.N.A.

{ SEVENTEEN }

I was assigned to D Hall with a very thorough C.N.A. I was also working with the nurse who had been my instructor. The first night of orientation was mainly spent learning the residents, assisting the C.N.A. and learning how to do the charting. Before entering a resident's room, she would explain any special precautions or requirements that would need to be met. One such resident was bed bound and could not breathe properly if laid flat for very long. Completing a full bed change had to be done very quickly. She also informed me to talk to him and assured me he would answer. I did as she had said, and he did answer me when I asked if he was okay. Until the third time I asked, his face was turning red, and he was not answering me. I immediately asked twice more, but no answer. I was about to become very concerned, when he looked at me and said, "If you bitches would hurry up I would fine!". He thought this was hilarious, pulling this on the new C.N.A. Me, not so much! But working that hall over the next year, he and I had plenty of laughs, picking on each other. The first night of orientation went well.

The second night, at the beginning of our shift the C.N.A. informed me that we would switch roles. I would take the lead and she would assist me. It was going well, and we had finished our fourth set of rounds (which were done every two hours). I asked her if it would be okay if I took a smoke break, she told me to go ahead, so I headed outside. I had barely sat down when she came rushing out the door telling me that I was needed at the nurse's station, and she was gone just as quickly.

I immediately headed inside, as I approached the nurse's station, I realized everyone (staff) was gathered around. My first thought was 'if we're having a party, I didn't get the memo'! The nurse for the other side of the building told me he needed me on B Hall, nothing out of the ordinary, if we were not busy on our hall, we were to assist on another one. He also informed me he was coming with me. I immediately thought what I did wrong that he needed to observe me performing. As we headed down the hall, he tells me, "Here's the thing _____ we have a deceased.". I replied, "No, here's the thing _____ second night of orientation, I have never done this.". This conversation was taking place as the C.N.A. (from my hall) is following us repeating, "I can't do this, I can't go in that room.". First off, no one had asked her too. Secondly, I was trying to listen to the nurse tell me what needed to be done. So, I turned and told her, "We heard you the first twenty times, go back to D Hall!".

We entered the room, the resident was sitting in her recliner as if she were only sleeping. The nurse informed me the first thing we needed to do was transfer her to the bed. I must point out, she was not a small woman. He instructed me to get her ankles, he would get under her arms and on the count of three we would move her to the bed. One, Two, Three _____ or Not! I gained a whole new perspective for 'dead' weight! We completed the transfer with extra help.

All I can say is Thank God for the C.N.A. from the other hall. She knew what needed to be done and assisted me. The C.N.A. who was working that hall had left the room (and the building)! Never to be seen again. Some can handle death, for others it is a deciding point, it is when they figure out this job is not for them.

EIGHTEEN

Working as a C.N.A., every shift brings with it challenges. Mis- communications should not be one of them, but it can and does occur anytime there are people working together. A new Med-Aid had begun working with us and was covering a hall in the capacity of C.N.A. I stopped her by the nurse's station and reminded her to check a resident's I's and O's (input and output). She gave me a strange look and went into the breakroom. I immediately thought, 'She is a Med-Aid and does not know what I's and O's are?'. She came out of the break room laughing and explained to me she thought I had said 'eyes and nose'! We both were laughing when I told her, "Yes, hold their nose and count, see how long it takes for their eyes to open wide!"

One challenge I faced was putting compression hose on an actual resident. The only experience I had was with the mannequin in class. It was (putting it nicely) like stretching toddler size tights over a watermelon! But after about forty minutes I had succeeded. And I thought the mannequin with the floppy ankle was difficult!

As C.N.A.'s we are trained to encourage our residents to do (what they are capable of) for themselves. The challenge comes when you know full well what they can do, but they insist that they cannot. You do not argue with them, you simply assist them with the task. Then the very next day you enter their room and they are doing exactly what they said they could not!

One difficult challenge comes when they should no longer transfer themselves from their wheelchair to bed (or vice versa). Now they have become a fall risk, and you must keep a closer eye on them. Especially those with dementia, who still believe they can do things for themselves.

{ NINETEEN }

Lessons learned through the fire service also helped while working at the nursing home. One such lesson I fell back on many times was improvise, adapt, and overcome. Sometimes you just have to go with the flow.

When responding to a resident's call light you never knew what you would encounter. For the most part they simply needed a glass of water, snack, or assistance in some way. Then there were those that were just seeking attention, or as with dementia patients, were lost in another time and place. Others were just wanting some company, particularly those who (for the most part) were bed bound and had very few, if any, visitors.

One such resident seeking attention, was Mrs. D. I responded to her call light and she told me she could not breathe, she had no trouble telling me this. I notified the nurse and proceeded to check her oxygen level, which was ninety-eight percent. Not a minute after leaving her room, her call light was back on. Again, she said she could not breathe, even though she was not demonstrating any difficulties and had no history of breathing issues. I told her, "You are talking to me just fine, you are breathing.". No more call light that night apart from her actually needing assistance.

Another 'attention seeker' got out of his bed, pressed the call button, and laid down on the fall mat on the floor next to his bed. If he had fallen in that position his call button would not have been within reach. I answered his call light and he tells me he thinks he broke his hip. I called for the nurse, who came and checked him and returned to the nurse's station to call for an ambulance (which is protocol). I stayed with him telling him, "Lay perfectly still, do not move.", making sure he stayed still. When the paramedics arrived with a backboard and gurney, he told them, "I can get back in bed if you help me.". With a 'broken' hip?! They transported him to the emergency room, and brought him back within two hours, no broken hip. But he did get attention!

When a resident is in another place and time due to dementia, you just go with the flow and try to redirect them. It does no good to correct or argue with them. Whatever place and time in their life they are, in their mind it is very real. For instance, if they believe it is 1942, telling them it is 2018 makes no sense to them, how can it be 2018 if you believe it is 1942? Upon entering one such resident's room to assist her getting ready for bed, it became very clear that she believed me to be her stepmother. She became emotional and thanked me profusely for 'staying and raising all of us kids.' I helped her to bed and knowing I had other call lights to answer I simply told her I had to go get the other 'kids' to bed. She told me good night as I turned her lamp off and left her room. I never did know how many 'kids' I 'raised'. This 'sweet' lady was also known to tell you, "I cannot hear you.". Her hearing was perfectly fine! But if you leaned down closer to talk to her, you might just end up with a black eye or a busted lip!

So many times, they go back to a time in their life when they were younger. To a happier time when they had small children, a career, or hobbies they enjoyed. One such resident, Mrs. L. would wheel herself up to the nurse's station late at night. On one particular night she came up to me asking to use the phone. She needed to call her father and let him know where she was. The nurse looked up at me from behind the nurse's station and whispered, "That's going to be a long-distance phone call." Doing my best to keep a straight face, I assured Mrs. L. he had been called and told she was staying with us. As she turned her wheelchair to go back to her room, I asked her how old she was, she answered me, "Eighteen". She was in her late eighties.

Many times, they suffer from sundowners, they have no concept of what time of day or night it is. Mrs. L. wheeled up to the nurse's station very late at night wanting a hamburger. We tried to explain to her that the kitchen was closed until the next morning. But she was persistent, asking how much a hamburger cost. C.N.A. Debra, without missing a beat, replied, "$14.99"! Mrs. L. thought for a moment and said, "Do you have any sandwiches?". I figured she must have thought a sandwich was bound to be cheaper. I told Debra, "I hope that price includes a drink."!

Mrs. H. was another resident who would wheel herself up to the nurse's station (almost nightly) asking to use the phone. She needed to call her husband (long since deceased) to tell him to come pick her up. We would explain that the phones did not work after ten p.m. (of course they did). The phones would be back on at eight a.m. (our shift ended at six a.m.!) This usually worked and she would go back to her room.

TWENTY

As a C.N.A. we are taught different methods of redirecting the residents when need be, without upsetting them or the incident escalating. You also learn a lot from C.N.A.'s that have been on the job longer. Their experiences can help you with little tips and secrets you might not have known otherwise. Sometimes you must be creative in your approach and think on your feet.

There was a resident who had suffered a major head trauma, effecting his short-term memory. The main thing that would upset him was being told he 'had' to do something. It only succeeded in making him really mad. One morning during our final rounds, I heard his voice across the building. He was very agitated, cussing the C.N.A. on his hall, and standing with a gate belt around him. When I intervened, his wheelchair was about three feet behind him. I approached him calmly, asking what was wrong. He told me, "He's an idiot.", it was clear the male C.N.A. had made him mad. As I talked to him, I slowly moved his wheelchair up behind him. The C.N.A. kept telling me, "He is not going to sit down.". Ignoring him, I continued to calmly talk to the resident. Thanks to C.N.A. Rhonda, I knew the secret of the cookies! I told him if he would sit down in his chair for me, we would go get cookies. He replied, "Cookies are good.". I told him I knew where they kept the cookies and if he sat down, we would go get some. He promptly sat down, and I pushed his wheelchair down the hall. We went for cookies and left a surprised C.N.A. standing in the middle of the hall, speechless!

TWENTY-ONE

After almost a year on D Hall, a coworker approached me to see if I wanted to switch halls. Her hall was one of the more demanding and she needed a break. I agreed, and with permission we switched. I was now working with the male nurse. Let me clarify, I have no problem working with a male nurse, but he had a gruff voice, and my first impression of him was he would be a very demanding, by the book, no-nonsense nurse. Was I ever wrong! After he (jokingly) picked on me that first night, we both learned something about the other. I learned he was not so hard-nosed, and he learned I could hold my own and 'pick' back.

We made a good working connection almost immediately. I paid attention and quickly learned what he expected of me as his C.N.A. He would also assist me with my duties when I asked for help. If I reported that a resident was not responding in a normal way, or I 'believe something is wrong', he would stop what he was doing and come with me to check. He had begun his career as a C.N.A. and understood our position at work. We worked well together for two and half years on that hall.

As I took care of my residents, being new to that hall, C.N.A. Rhonda helped me learn their likes and dislikes (it had been her hall and she knew the residents well). I also talked with them, inquiring about their lives, children, if they had worked, what type of job they had had. Of course, they asked me about my life, children, and my dogs. This exchange gave me the chance to know them better and in turn it helped me to provide better personalized care.

I had told one resident about my spoiled rotten dachshund and had shown her a picture of him when she asked me what he looked like. From then on, every time I was on shift, she would ask me, "How's my boy?". I would tell her he was spoiled as ever, she always told me, "Well you know who did it.". Implying it was me that had spoiled him! She always gave me little packages of M & M's, snack crackers, or cookies, not for me! But to take home to 'her' boy.

Even though we were advised against getting too attached to our residents, we all did. We all had our favorites.

I had one lady on my hall, Mrs. W. who would loan me books to read from her 'collection'. We both liked true crime and mysteries. She loved reading as much as I did, and would excitedly tell me, "You need to read this one when I finish it.". I wish I could tell her now that I am writing a book, but sadly she passed away.

I had another lady that would always make sure I had something to eat. I always assured her that I had brought my dinner with me and I had plenty. She would tell me to hold my pocket on my scrub top open and she would pour jellybeans in it, to give me the 'energy' that she figured I needed.

There was one resident who after talking to him, thought I really needed to be married. He constantly asked me when I was going to get married again. Each time I would tell him I had been divorced for twelve years and I was perfectly happy, just me and my dogs. But for a year he was relentless. He even suggested I should visit a church in Abilene, Texas, 'it had a nice young people's group'! Okay, I will take the 'young' part as a compliment. Another suggestion he gave me was to join a square-dancing club, I could just see me in all those petticoats _____ or Not!

One evening I answered his call light and out of nowhere he asked me if I was Mormon! I told him, "No, I was raised Southern Baptist.". Unaware that my nurse had come in behind me, passing meds, I hear him say, "Just like me.". Well that opened a whole new conversation for the resident! He proceeded to say we should get married. Before I could say anything, my nurse tells him, "We are."! It does not happen very often, but I was speechless. It was the last thing I expected him to say! I immediately walked out into the hall, waiting there until he came out of that room. Then, I was anything but speechless! I asked him, "What the hell were you thinking?! Now he will bug me even more!". He replied, "Just watch, now he will leave you alone.". I was not convinced of that and told him to just remember, he started this! The next night I wore my engagement ring (from a prior proposal). As soon as I answered the resident's call light that evening, he told me how wonderful he thought it was that I was getting married. I showed him the 'rock' on my hand and said, "Well yeah, did you see this ring?". He of course, said, it was nice but not a good reason for getting married. I stated again, "But, did you see this ring?!". At that point I think he gave up on me, he never mentioned me and marriage in the same sentence again! Besides, my nurse already has a fantastic wife.

{ TWENTY-TWO }

As I have stated before, it is good to have a sense of humor in this line of work (or any job for that matter). By the third twelve-hour night shift in a row, we got silly and things got funny. You start seeing the humor in everything!

I had a resident on my hall that would hold his head up off the pillow when I would lower the head of his bed at night. I would adjust his pillows to his liking and would calmly tell him he could lay his head down. He would inform me that he could not lay his head down because his neck was too short! After having this conversation with him one evening (one of many) I left his room, shaking my head. Then it came to me! I approached my nurse and told him I knew what Mr. W. suffered from. He gave me a very puzzled look and I told him, "Mr. W. has 'short-a-neck-a-nitis'! My nurse spit his drink, and we both started laughing. Who knows? There might be a grant available to do further research into this 'condition'. And I have 'heard' the best research area is in the Caribbean!

I had another resident inform me she could not have tea _____ it affected her medication. Thinking there might be something to it, I went and asked the nurse. She gave me that look, you know the one, that 'what the heck are you talking about' look. I was told there was no effect on medication, she just wanted Kool-Aid instead of tea!

Another resident (suffering from dementia) offered one of the other C.N.A.'s a job _____ because "the room service at this hotel sucks!".

As I stated, it is good to have a sense of humor, but it is also important to do so in a way that the residents do not think you are laughing AT them. I had very few residents that did not have a sense of humor and would joke and laugh with me. Some even made fun of themselves or their situation. Unlike some that came to the nursing facility for rehabilitation after an accident or surgery, or those there because family could no longer take care of them at home, there were those that had made the decision to live there on their own. Those residents knew that they had come to a point in their life when they needed more assistance and could no longer live on their own.

{ TWENTY-THREE }

You learn all kinds of lessons working at a nursing home, and not all pertain to the job itself. I learned to keep air freshener on my hall, not necessarily due to the residents (many were incontinent). It was mainly for my benefit because of my nurse! Without going into too much detail, let me just say he liked boiled eggs, cabbage, and chili. He thought it was funny, *covering nose* me, not so much!

After one such 'incident' in a resident's room, the resident's wife walked in and took him to the bathroom. She thought he had had an accident! Which of course, he had not.

On another occasion of my nurse 'fumigating' my hall, he was at the med cart when a resident walked by him. The resident exclaimed, "What is that smell?". I just pointed at my nurse. When he came back by heading back to his room, he had to pass behind the nurse and he told him, "Don't crop dust me Charles!". We were both laughing at the remark! And I proceeded to grab my air freshener and spray my hall (and him)!

TWENTY-FOUR

Working in a nursing home, you took care of residents with dementia, Alzheimer's, bi-polar and other behaviors. There were those that liked to 'wander'. Only twice in four and a half years did we have to conduct a room to room search and search the grounds. The resident involved was always found and taken back to their room. One lady was found out front of the facility, digging in one of the large potted plants. She told us she was cleaning up her garden. We told her that since it was getting dark, she needed to come in and get cleaned up, she could 'work' in her 'garden' tomorrow. She dusted her hands off and went back inside with us.

Another resident, Mrs. R. L., liked to try to go outdoors, she was what we referred to as a 'Curious Cat'. She had a bracelet put on that would set off the exit door alarm when she got too close. Each time you would redirect her away from the door, she would call you a jack-a$$! I went up to R.N. Barbara one night and told her, "I want my crown!". She looked at me puzzled, so I explained, "Mrs. R.L. called me the jack-a$$ of jack-a$$es! I want my crown." We both got a good laugh from that.

We had one resident that had to be transferred to a mental facility after an incident. When she returned, after six weeks, I made it a point to welcome her back. The next morning I was making my last rounds of the shift, getting resident dressed and ready for breakfast, when I see her pass by the room I was in, headed for the end of the hall (where an exit door was located). Before I could get to her, she pulled the fire alarm, she then proceeded calmly back down the hall and into her room. An alarm being activated meant that the doors to the hallways automatically closed, alarms rang continuous, and the nurse had to call the dispatcher and report that it was a false alarm, set off by a resident. He then reset the system. The only conclusion for this behavior, she wanted to go back to the behavioral facility. She liked it there, where there was more one on one attention.

Most residents had their own cell phones in their room and for the most part this was not an issue. However, with some, it could become a problem. Such was the case with one lady who call 9-1-1, stating her 'emergency', she was 'being held against her will, and we had stolen her shoes'. She was at our facility for rehabilitation due to hip surgery. The dispatcher, per protocol, called the nurse's station to inform the nurse of the phone call. She also pushed her call button one evening and when I answer it, she told me someone was outside her window. I checked the window, closed the blinds and curtain and assured her there was no one outside. A few nights later, I was checking the hall, while the other C.N.A. was at lunch, and found this same resident on the floor by her bed. I immediately called for the nurse and returned to her side. When he entered the room, he asked her if she could turn over onto her back, placing a pillow under her head, we assisted her in turning onto her back. It became obvious (visually) that she had re-broke her hip. When asked what happened and how she fell out of bed, she told us, 'they' had told her to get up! There was no 'they' in her room.

There were those residents that when we answered their call light would immediately begin yelling at us. I would calmly ask what they needed, and if they continued to yell, I would leave the room, telling them I would return when they stopped yelling at me. This usually worked, as it surprised them that I would just leave. Their call light would come back on and I would go answer it. In the few minutes I had been out of their room, their attitude would have changed. One gentleman told me, upon re-entering his room, "I am so glad to see you, I know when you are here the job will be done right"! Three minutes earlier, he was yelling at me and threatening to 'fire' me! He also believed that he 'owned' the facility.

Another such incident occurred when I answered the call light of another resident, I entered the room and inquired as to what he needed. He proceeded to tell me, "You damn well know what I want.". I proceeded to calmly tell him that it was not necessary to talk to me in that way, and that, no I could not read minds and did not know what he needed unless he told me. He again started cussing and telling me there was nothing I could do about it. I informed him, "Yes, there is, I can walk out of your room, go inform the nurse that I will not be answering your call light and why, and let one of the other C.N.A.'s answer it. However, they are all very busy so it will be a little while before they can answer your call light.". Again, he started cussing at me, I walked out of the room and let the nurse know the conversation I had just had. His call light came back on, I did go answer it, and his demeanor had changed. It was now, 'yes and thank you'.

There was one couple that had come to the nursing home within a week of each other. Naturally, being married they were put into the same room. That proved to be a mistake, due to him constantly telling the nurse that his wife was dying (in front of her!). Because of arguing and other issues, they were separated to different rooms, on different halls. After she was admitted to the hospital to be set up for dialysis, I am not sure what occurred, but she no longer listened to him, and in fact would tell him to 'shut up'. They were again placed in a room together. He was in the common room one evening watching television and I passed by, I just happen to hear the commercial that was on. It was discussing a contraceptive that is placed under the skin in the arm. About an hour later, he pushed his call light and when I answered it, he proceeded to tell me, "I know what is killing my wife.", while she was lying in bed across the room. He then proceeded to tell me about the commercial he had seen. She was there during this whole conversation. I told him, "No sir, what you saw was about a contraceptive.". That is when she laughed and commented, "I haven't needed that in a very long time!". I left the room before I started laughing.

{ TWENTY-FIVE }

Anyone who has worked in a nursing home, or the medical field, will understand. Family members can be a blessing _____ or a Nightmare!

There were many family members who were very appreciative of the work and care we provided, and they showed it. They were thankful of the extra care we gave when their loved ones were facing their final days.

On the other side of the coin, were the ones who became a nightmare when they came to visit. The ones who you looked forward to the end of their visit. Family members who pushed the call light more than the resident. When I would answer such a call light, I would address the resident. If indeed they needed something, I would take care of them. I would barely leave the room and the call light was back on. The family member would even tell me they pressed it, and then proceed to tell me what their mother/father needed. At least what they thought was needed.

Working in a nursing home. Death is inevitable. We strived to take care of their needs and keep them comfortable in their final days. In one such situation the family asked me the strangest question I had ever been asked. I had just finished providing care for their mother and stepped into the hallway. Her daughters followed me out of the room and said they had a question. I told them I would answer it if I could, if not I would gladly get the nurse. One daughter spoke up and asked, "How long is this going to take?". Stunned for a moment, my first thought was 'does Mom have valuables you can't wait to get?!'. I answered, "It can take hours, days, or weeks. It is not up to us. *pointing skyward*, it is up to Him (God).". I turned and walked away. I told the nurse about the conversation I had just had, and how I answered their question. She simply said, "Good answer.".

For the most part I enjoyed talking to the family members. I also learned about my residents from many of those conversations. There were times I would approach them and ask about my resident's life, especially if they suffered from dementia, and were unable to tell me themselves.

Mrs. L. would sit near the nurse's station nightly. She constantly would tell us, 'the horses need to be fed' or 'the horses need to be put in the barn'. Yet there were no pictures or anything referencing horses in her room. On one occasion when her son came to visit, I asked him if she had horses at some time. He smiled and shared with me that his mother and father had lived and worked on a ranch. That she also had the first all-female riding club to perform at the big prison rodeo. It all made sense, her reference to taking care of the horses.

Another resident's son who had come to visit asked me if she had ever told me how she had met his father. I politely told him she had never mentioned it (she had dementia). He went on to tell me the story of how they met in Maine. She lived there at the time, his father was in port, as he served in the military. They met at the ice rink where she was skating with her girlfriends and saw him across the ice. She told her friends that she was going to meet that tall sailor. He had gone to try ice skating, being from Texas, he had never attempted it. She skated across to him, where she whirled and twirled on her ice skates, and he fell, on the ice _____ and for her! She was a figure skater and her son still has her ice skates from all those years ago.

After this conversation, a remark she had made to me and another C.N.A. made sense. She had told us as we were leaving her room one evening, "You girls be careful tonight, those sailors are in town."!

For many I took care of there was only a slight glimpse into their past. Some had no visitors or family. With those who did, working nights, we rarely met them. For one such gentleman, all I knew was that he was a veteran. I never was able to find out what branch of the military he served with, or what his rank and/or job had been. But there were evenings that I would catch a glimpse, if only for a few minutes (due to dementia).

The first interaction I had with him was in going into his room to see if he was ready to get into bed, he had to have assistance. He immediately looked up at me and asked, "Young lady where is your cap?". Again, my age helped me out, I knew he was referring to a Nurse's cap, back when they wore a white nurse's uniform with white hose and a cap. I understood immediately what he was referring too and told him, "Oh, I must have left it at the Nurse's station, I better go get it.". That set him at ease, I left his room for a couple of minutes and when I returned, he was ready to get into bed.

In another instance, I entered his room to check on him. He handed me a stack of papers, old calendar pages, junk mail and such. As he handed them to me, he told me, "These need to be destroyed. They cannot get into the wrong hands.". I simply replied, "Yes sir, I will take care of them.". I walked out and tossing them into my trash can, I wondered, what he did and if he was able, what stories he could tell. On a particularly stormy night, he heard the thunder and rain. He looked at me and said, "The execution will have to be postponed, not a good night for it."! Was it just his mind playing tricks on him? Or, what position had he been in while in the service? If his memory had not been affected, would he have told about his experiences? I think not. I remember my grandfather always saying, "Loose lips sink ships.".

{ TWENTY-SIX }

Dealing with death is part of the job when working at a nursing home. For far too many, the nurses and C.N.A.'s are their only 'family'. We are the only ones with them in their final days. If you have ever heard someone say 'they come in threes', it is very true. Sometimes it can come within weeks, days, or even hours.

Some nurses and C.N.A.'s can handle death better than others. It is part of the job, sometimes we knew it was just a matter of time, others came unexpectedly. There was one tradition I had never heard of prior to working in a nursing home. It goes that upon someone passing away, the window in their room needs to be opened. It is done to free the soul to move on to the afterlife. It is believed by some, that if the window remains closed the soul will be trapped and unable to move on. Old wives' tale or real _____ you decide.

There are times, even when faced with death, that a morbid sense of humor and/or a mouth with no filter is beneficial, okay, maybe not 'beneficial' but useful. I had a resident that was 'actively' passing, as it is referred too. I was taking vitals every ten minutes, C.N.A. Debra had accompanied me when I went to take a set of vitals. As we turned to leave the room there was a clean cut, nicely dressed young man standing at the doorway. Thinking he was possibly the gentleman's grandson, I politely asked, "May I help you?". That is when he very curtly replied, "I am from the funeral home, is he ready?". I calmly told him, "No, he is still breathing, but maybe you could take him for a ride around the block. I don't know, he might enjoy it."! Just a tad of sarcasm there. I then instructed him to go to the nurse's station and speak with them.

Debra looked at me in shock and said, "I cannot believe you just said that!". I simply shrugged my shoulders and replied, "What was I supposed to say?". Normally the funeral home is contacted after a person passes away. Maybe he was new at the job, a little overzealous?

Another incident involving funeral home employees occurred when a very large resident passed away. The funeral home employee entered the room pushing a gurney, about six-foot-long and a foot and half wide. I simply stated the obvious, that he would need a larger gurney. He replied, "This one will work, we don't have a bigger one.". That is when the filter fell of my mouth and referring to the deceased, I told him, "Have you seen him?". I got elbowed in the side from the nurse who was standing next to me! About that time the funeral home director walked into the room. He took one look and told his coworker to go get the larger gurney! I stated, "Isn't that what I just said?! He told us you did not have a larger one.", and got the elbow, for the second time.

Sometimes you just have to be blunt. After all, you are just stating the obvious, and saying what others are thinking.

In some cases, you never know how a resident will react to another resident's death and/or their spouse's (roommate) death. I had a resident pass away on my night off. The next evening when I came on duty, I figured I would have the extra 'job' of consoling her in her time of grief. However, as I approached my hall, she was coming out of the dining room, singing! She stopped me in the hall (anything but grief stricken) and proceeded to tell me, "My husband died last night, and I have a new roommate, she seems really nice and we've been having a good time today."! I always had the feeling that there was more to their story than met the eye. He always seemed to want to be in control.

{ TWENTY-SEVEN }

Ghost, spirits, and the Grim Reaper _____ do they really exist? You bet they do! Ask anyone who has ever worked at a nursing home. If they say 'no', they either did not work on the job long, or they are just trying to convince themselves they do not exist. Most all of the nurses and C.N.A.'s I worked with have had an experience at one time or another. All of us, on my rotation had times of experiencing the 'dark' shadow on our halls. Usually it coincided with a resident passing away. Or call lights would come on for a room that was no longer occupied.

The next night after one of my favorite residents had passed away, I had an experience with his spirit. I was standing at my kiosk doing my nightly charting, when suddenly (almost simultaneously) six call lights came on. One by one, I went to answer them. Each resident was sound asleep and obviously had not pushed the call light. Afterward, I was standing at the nurse's station, and I wondered (out loud), "What the heck is going on?". One of the nurses asked me what was wrong. I explained what had just occurred on my hall with the call lights, she laughed and told me, "It's just B.J. messing with you.". As I returned to my hall, I quietly told him, "B.J. knock it off!". It never occurred again.

At our facility there was a popcorn machine in the resident dining room. There was a gentleman (resident) that would go in the dining room, almost every night we worked, and make us bags of popcorn to snack on. After he passed away, occasionally, we would smell fresh popcorn. But none was being made.

At the end of each of the halls there was an emergency exit door with a full-length window beside it. On many occasions when we had a resident that was passing away a large white cat would sit outside the window of that hall, looking in. One nurse referred to the cat as the 'grim reaper'. Maybe, animals to seem to sense when someone is sick or dying.

These are only three of the many experiences I had during the three and a half years of working at the nursing home, not to mention stories and experiences shared by the nurses and C.N.A.'s.

TWENTY-EIGHT

You never know who you might be taking care of daily. Sometimes you learn from family members about their lives and accomplishments, as I did on several occasions. Other residents who passed away took their life stories with them, with no family to share their story. Other times, sadly, you learned from reading an obituary. Such was the case with one of my residents. His room was located next to our time clock. Each shift I worked, I would clock-in and then stop in his doorway to say hello and inquire as to how his day had been.

When he first came to the nursing home, I could not pronounce his name correctly, so he told me just call him 'Pops'. As soon as he would see me, he would tell me, "I asked God for an Angel, and here you are.". He repeated that to me throughout his stay there, I did not see it that way, I was just doing my job to the best of my ability.

Pops was a very humble man. Whenever I had a few minutes of time I would sit and visit with him. He told me how his Grandfather was a stonemason and had taught him the trade. He talked about how he had worked on some of the buildings in Austin, Texas.

I was working the night he passed away and a few days later I read his obituary in the local newspaper. I recalled him telling me how he had worked ON the buildings in Austin. He had never mentioned he had worked IN them! The following is a small excerpt from his obituary:

'Representative Birkner served in the 58th, 59th, and 60th Legislature of the Texas House of Representatives. He served on committees including Parks and Wildlife, Aeronautics, and Mental Health. He created the Head Start Program.'

As I mentioned previously, he was a very humble man. He never mentioned any of his accomplishments. As I sat outside at work, before our shift began, I read this to my co-workers. Afterward, in awe, I remarked, "It just goes to show you never know who you might be taking care of.". It was that remark in May of 2018 that lead to the idea of writing this book. I began making notes and a rough outline took form.

[TWENTY-NINE }

There have been so many lessons learned that carried over from fire service to C.N.A. to daily life. Being blessed to do what you love, even on a bad day, is a great accomplishment. If you love what you do, that is half the battle to keep going, even if there are those who try to discourage you. Luckily, I have had parents, family and friends that always encouraged me through all my endeavors.

I have learned how important teamwork can be. That having a fire-crew, co-workers, family and friends you can count on are an awesome part of work and life. Even though most everyone I know needs their paycheck, sometimes (no matter what your job is) there is more gratification than just the pay. Having been a C.N.A., it is not a position taken solely for the paycheck. It is caring for others when they can no longer care for themselves. It is doing what is right and what matters.

Knowing yourself is also important, as well as being honest with yourself. It is important to do whatever you choose to the best of your ability. Knowing when it is time to take the first step of ending one chapter and beginning a new one in your life is important. I have seen too many women fall into the way of thinking 'this is all I know how to do'. It is never too late to learn and step out of your 'comfort zone'. After all I had just turned 56 when I registered for the C.N.A. class and was going way beyond my comfort zone.

The step to my next life chapter came at age 59, when I turned in my written resignation to the Director of Nursing. I had not mentioned that I would be giving my two weeks' notice to anyone at work. When I turned it in, she read it (twice) and asked me if I was kidding. I assured her I was not, and she wished me well in my new

endeavor and told me that I would be greatly missed. Over the next two weeks I informed my co-workers and many of my residents that I would be leaving. I made promises to many that I would be back to visit.

On my next to last night I had just completed my last rounds at 5:30 a.m., when my nurse called me into a resident's room. He motioned toward Mr. A. (who was sitting in his recliner) and tells me, "He is still alive.". I looked at the nurse and replied, "That only means two things. I did not use any pillow 'therapy' last night and I still have a job.". Mr. A. looked from me to the nurse, who informed him, "I would watch her closely, tonight is her last shift here.". Mr. A. (among others) and I had joked with each other since the day he moved into the nursing home. I learned quickly which residents I could joke with and which ones it was better not too.

After leaving the nursing home, I 'hung up' my scrubs and went to the dogs _____ literally, going to work at the local Animal Shelter. Shortly after I began working there, one thing was confirmed, I like dogs more than most people! And the dogs did not have call lights!

As promised, I continued to go back and visit the residents at the nursing home. They loved hearing about and seeing pictures of the dogs in my care. I decided to set up a special visit. I spoke with the Director of the Shelter and the Administrator of the nursing home, and both gave their approval. Shelter dog, China, was going to visit the residents at the nursing home. She loved everyone and the residents loved her. Even though she had never been around wheelchairs, that we knew of, she had no issues with them. She approached the residents, whether in a wheelchair or not, expecting attention and giving love to them. Being on her best behavior, she even got treats from some of the nurses. As China and I were leaving, they did not tell me bye, but they all told China goodbye and to come back soon.

China did not get the chance to go back and visit. She was adopted and got her much deserved furever home. But I still stop by from time to time and visit my former residents. They always inquire as to how I am doing and what I am up too. Of course, they ask how my dogs are, and laugh when I tell them about fostering two puppies and my foster-fail Sam (from fostering to adoption in two days). I always have to have my phone with me since some ask to see pictures. It is good to see how they are doing and visit for a little while.

Only by strange coincidence was I able to set one of my former resident's mind at ease, when I was able to tell her that her poodle (she had to give up when she moved into the nursing home) which had been at the shelter had gone to a senior dog rescue, and was assured a good home.

*As of the writing of this book I have not been able to go visit in a while, since the Covid-19 pandemic. Nursing homes were closed to visitors in March 2020. But as soon as all of this is over, I will be going back to visit.

{ THIRTY }

The following tribute was posted on Facebook by Songbird Lodge Nursing and Rehabilitation Center, in memory of Debra Perry. She passed away in 2020 during the writing of this book. She was an awesome C.N.A., and a great friend, and an inspiration to all who knew her.

'This job is hard, and the days can be long. So, we make friends with our coworkers, they pull us through the long shifts, let us cry when we lose residents and we rejoice together when they get to go home. Without that camaraderie I am not sure how we could work in this industry for long. So, it is especially hard to lose a beloved co-worker who in turn becomes family. We lost a dear friend and co-worker, Debra Perry. We pray that her family is surrounded by the light of love that Debra projected from her sweet smile and loving personality. Debra will always have a place in our hearts at Songbird Lodge.'

Debra, you will always be loved, and you will always be remembered.

ACKNOWLEDGEMENTS

To my family, for always believing in me and giving me the encouragement to push forward, even when times got tough.

Tom Bourbon, the first Fire Chief I worked with, for encouraging me to become a Wildland Firefighter.

Chris Weber, a great Fire Chief, leader, and friend. He believed in my capabilities even when there were times, I questioned myself. He always led by example, not just orders and/or assignments.

Mona Murdock, fellow firefighter, friend, and partner in 'crime'. Thank you for keeping the sarcasm and coffee flowing.

Dam Volunteer Fire Department crew for the comradery on and off the fire line. For dog-sitting (you know who you are) when I needed a vacation. Brandon Graves, for shoveling 'snow' in my living room when Chainsaw (my pup) decided she was mad at me for leaving her at home, and de-stuffed my throw pillows.

The Texas Forest Service instructors, too many to name, who taught me so much in and out of the classroom. There were so many life lessons I learned from being in the fire service that I carry with me in daily life.

The following people who played such a big role in my years as a Certified Nurse Assistant.

Pam Martin, the first Director of Nursing I worked under. She will always hold a special place in my heart. During my clinicals she made it possible for me to be with my mom when she passed away, and still complete my clinicals.

Earlene Shaw, L.V.N., a fantastic instructor, nurse and friend. Thank you for providing 'goat' therapy when work and life got a little on the crazy side.

Charles Harvey, L.V.N., for never being too busy to answer questions or help me when I needed assistance. For teaching me how important it was to always keep air freshener on hand when working with him! And the amazing handmade candies he brought with him at Christmas.

To the C.N.A.'s who worked my rotation and taught me so much.

Debra Perry, for breaking me in and helping me learn lessons not covered in the classroom. For providing laughs, even when it was at her expense. I never knew anyone could blush that deep shade of pink! Sadly, Debra passed away while I was writing this book. She will be missed by many.

Rhonda Denson, for keeping the coffee flowing and sharing the crayons! Most importantly for teaching me tips and little secrets to help deal with difficult residents.

Rebecca Gregory, an awesome and hardworking C.N.A. She was always available to lend a hand, an ear to vent too, and she loves coffee (and bubble tea) as much as I do.

Tiffany Perrin, who is a great and compassionate C.N.A. When she felt left out because she was the only one on our shift not

taking a smoke break, I bought her a pack
_____ of candy cigarettes.

   To all the nurses, R.N.'s and L.V.N.'s, I worked with periodically. They always appreciated the C.N.A.'s and the work we did.

   To the day shift C.N.A.'s, not sure how they did it, but the one's that worked my hall always made me coming on shift easier.

   To all my co-workers on my rotation, thank you for helping me keep what little sanity I had (after being in the fire service). Especially those times when I was asking myself, "What the hell was I thinking, becoming a C.N.A.?". I was blessed to work with such a great crew.